FREDDIE M...

A Life from Beginning to End

Table of Contents

Introduction

Freddie Mercury was the ultimate rock star. He had a natural sense of timing and theatrics—some would say that he was made for the stage. But where Freddie came from, the life of a rockstar was about as far removed from experience as possible. He was born on the East African island of Zanzibar (part of modern-day Tanzania) on September 5, 1946, and his name at birth wasn't Freddie Mercury—it was Farrokh Bulsara.

Freddie was a nickname that Farrokh was given by his classmates while he was attending boarding school in India. In all, he would spend about eight years of his childhood in India away from his family. It was here that he first learned how to play the piano, having started his lessons at the mere age of seven. Some of his school friends from these years recognized Freddie's musical talents early on and claimed that he had "an uncanny ability to listen to the radio and replay what he heard on piano." Besides music, Freddie also proved to be an accomplished athlete. He joined the boxing team, became the school champion of table tennis, and even at one point won an award for best all-around athlete.

Although Freddie was born in faraway Zanzibar, he actually came from a family of Parsi Indians. The Parsi Indians were Persian descendants who had fled to India during the Muslim/Arab conquest of Persia (modern-day Iran) in the seventh century. Prior to this Islamic takeover, Persia was the land of Zoroastrianism and classic eastern mysticism. Freddie's parents, Bomi and Jer Bulsara, hailed from this rich tradition and imparted their Zoroastrian wisdom onto their son. These Zoroastrian roots, though not openly spoken of much by Freddie, would subtly emerge in some of the imagery of his songs. The 1974 hit "Seven Seas of Rhye" perhaps best expresses this sentiment, as some claim its lyrics allude to the mystical journey of the prophet Zoroaster.

Mystical or not, Freddie Mercury's own precocious childhood had come to an end some ten years earlier in 1964 when Zanzibar was rocked by a brutal and bloody revolution.

Chapter One

Early Life in Zanzibar

"I always knew I was a star and now, the rest of the world seems to agree with me."

—Freddie Mercury

Zanzibar is part of a group of islands in the Indian Ocean just east of the modern-day African nation of Tanzania. For such a small piece of real estate, Zanzibar has an incredibly complex history. Since ancient times, the ownership of Zanzibar has shifted hands on numerous occasions. It was at various points an outpost for Sumerians, Assyrians, Egyptians, and Phoenicians. Zanzibar was also a crossroads for Indians and Persians until it was ultimately conquered by Arab/Muslim forces in 1698.

The land was then controlled by outside Islamic powers until Zanzibar became an independent sultanate in 1858, ushering in a period of Arab home rule run by the local sultan. The ownership of Zanzibar would see another change in 1890 when the British became involved, and although not taking over the island outright, they significantly reduced the power of the reigning sultan by making Zanzibar a British protectorate.

This made Zanzibar a constitutional monarchy patterned off the British system, with the sultan remaining in place as monarch. This arrangement would last until the British pulled out in December of 1963, granting Zanzibar full independence. It would be less than two months later that the land was rocked by a revolution. The seed of discord that led to this tumult was the fact that Zanzibar had been ruled by an Arab minority for decades, while the African majority on the island were routinely kept out of positions of power.

Fed up with their second-class treatment, a group of African militants staged an uprising in which they stormed police stations, killed several police officers, and stocked up on all the weapons they could find. This was the beginning of a bloody revolt that would send many Zanzibar's residents—Freddie Mercury's family included—into full-blown flight from the country.

Oppressed or not, the militants were absolutely brutal in their revenge against the more affluent minority. Once the police were put out of business, bloodthirsty bands roamed the countryside, breaking into the houses of Arabs, Persians, Indians, and the like, killing, robbing, and raping those they found inside. Realizing that this was no place to raise a family, Freddie's mother and father packed a couple of suitcases with whatever essential items would fit, and with Freddie and his little sister Kashmira in tow, they booked a flight to Heathrow Airport.

Freddie's father was in the fortunate position of having worked for British interests in Zanzibar, and with the utility of his British passport in hand, he was able to broker an escape for his loved ones to the British Isles. It was this sudden turn of fate that would send a young Freddie Mercury on a trajectory destined for superstardom.

Many have wondered why Freddie Mercury didn't speak much of his Zanzibar roots. As one can imagine, this tragedy gave him more than enough reason to keep quiet about it. Today, perhaps things would be a little different, as artists are keener to embrace the tragedies of their past. For Freddie, however, he simply wished to compartmentalize the trauma and move forward as best he could.

Freddie's family ended up settling in a modest home on London's west side. Despite the chaos and turmoil that had brought him to the shores of Great Britain, it's said that Freddie was fairly eager for the new start that Britain would provide. Being an immigrant from an exotic land like Zanzibar didn't exactly make things easy for him among Londoners of the 1960s, but he tried his best to adapt.

Freddie was almost 18 years old at the time, and his parents were hoping that he would set his sights on a solid career path, such as being some sort of civil servant, an attorney, or perhaps even an accountant. His father was already doing the latter, having landed a job as an accountant for a catering company in London. But Freddie didn't like the sound of any of that. To appease his parents, the listless teenager would occasionally fill out some job applications, but only half-heartedly—all the while dreaming of doing something much more spectacular than crunching numbers in an office.

Around this time, Freddie came up with the idea that he wanted to go to art school. It wasn't so much because he wanted to paint or create any specific kind of art; as it was, he believed that art school was the place where he could meet true artists. It seems that he first came to this conclusion as a boy back in Zanzibar when he read up on all the famous musicians that had met in art school. Many prominent groups such as The Beatles, The Who, and others did indeed meet at art school. So it was that Freddie set his sights on London's Ealing Technical College & School of Art. He hoped that this little Bohemian enclave of art and culture would be the environment in which he would meet some like minds to help him advance his career.

The only trouble was, his disrupted education in Zanzibar wasn't quite up to snuff to attend Ealing, and he would have to go to a less prestigious polytechnic school first. It was at London's Isleworth Polytechnic school that Freddie would enroll in September of 1964, taking what is known as an art foundation course. It was with his entry into this little-known polytechnic school that Freddie would begin to lay down the foundation of his rock and roll roots.

Chapter Two

Life at Art School

"I'm very emotional; I think I may go mad in several years' time."

—Freddie Mercury

Freddie was a fairly shy student during his two-year tenure at Isleworth Polytechnic. The only real clue as to what he may have been like in those days is a video that has surfaced, dated from 1965, which he and a few of his friends had made as a kind of avant-garde silent film. In this brief sequence, a quiet and somewhat embarrassed Freddie Mercury is seen sitting on a park bench and gesticulating in what must have been prearranged movements. He is indeed painfully shy, but even then, the few movements he made seem to reveal a theatrical flair.

Freddie had signed on at Isleworth Polytechnic with the full intent of transferring to Ealing Art College once his grades were up to par, and in these efforts, he was successful.

Freddie was accepted at Ealing in the fall of 1966. Upon enrollment at Ealing, a 20-year-old Freddie Mercury moved into his own apartment on the west side of London. Art school in those days were havens for budding musicians wishing to make it big.

It was around this time that Freddie Mercury first became aware of the sounds of an American turned British resident by the name of Jimi Hendrix. Rock and roll icon Hendrix had come to Britain on September 23, 1966, right around the time Freddie was getting started at Ealing. From the first moment Freddie found out about Hendrix, he was absolutely mesmerized. He loved the music, but he also loved the image and persona of Hendrix as a whole. Jimi Hendrix a man of many diverging backgrounds and cast himself as a roving gypsy. Freddie Mercury, who himself was a transplant in Britain, could most certainly relate.

Freddie soon began to emulate Hendrix in every way he could; he tried to dress like him, he practiced singing like him, and he sketched drawings of the rockstar whenever he had some downtime. You could safely say that Freddie was a little bit obsessed with Jimi—in fact, it almost cost him his place at Ealing. The principal, James

Drew, took note that Freddie had been cutting class and held him to task for it. Principal Drew didn't know the reason, but much of the time, Freddie was going out to Hendrix concerts.

Freddie, alarmed that his coursework might be in jeopardy, managed to convince the principal to allow him to stay the course and got himself switched out of the fashion design classes he was taking for coursework in graphic art instead. It was Freddie's move over to graphic design that would prove pivotal, for it was here that he would meet the likes of Tim Staffell, Nigel Foster, and Chris Smith, with whom he would forge his first incarnations of rock music.

Tim Staffell was already a fairly experienced musician at this point and was performing for a band called 1984. Staffell sang and played harmonica for the group while a talented young musician by the name of Brian May helmed the guitar. Brian May would later become the iconic lead guitarist of Queen, and even back then, his fingers knew how to work a fretboard.

The group had some marginal success and were eventually deemed solid enough to open for none other than Freddie's hero, Jimi Hendrix. Freddie must have been elated to have a friend in such close proximation to Jimi, and although it's not known for certain, it's believed that he was most likely in the crowd for the event.

The group would eventually break up in 1968, but Staffell and May would remain in contact with each other, and Freddie and Staffell would remain good friends as well. Being Staffell's friend, Freddie followed all the latest developments of his music career very closely. He was right on the scene in the fall of 1968 when Staffell and May formed a new music group in which Staffell played bass and sang, and May lent his considerable talent on the electric guitar.

This time around, Staffell and May were determined to form a trio, and as such they began seeking out a drummer. Like many musicians did back then, and some still do today, in order to find one, they simply put up a makeshift poster with their contact details. This "drummer wanted" notice was promptly plastered on a bulletin board in the halls of Imperial College which Brian May was attending at the time.

They received a lot of inquiries for their efforts, but most of those that tried out either lacked talent or just didn't mesh well enough with May and Staffell's style. The real breakthrough came when a man by the name of Les Brian waltzed on by, snatched up the notice, and took it home with him. Les wasn't actually a drummer himself, but he knew someone that would be perfect for the job—his roommate, Roger Taylor.

Unlike all of the other drummers who had come before, as soon as May and Staffell heard Taylor, they knew that he was the percussionist they were looking for. Brian May would later recall that "just the sound of him tuning his drums was better than I had heard from anyone before. It was amazing."

Roger fit in with May and Staffell, and they intuitively knew that this was their guy. They now thought that their new band was complete—but little did they know that a man who would eventually call himself Freddie Mercury was still waiting in the wings.

Chapter Three

Musical Endeavors Before Queen

*"A concert is not a live rendition of our album.
It's a theatrical event."*

—Freddie Mercury

The band that Brian May, Tim Staffell, and Roger Taylor were in the process of forming frequently jammed out at Taylor's apartment. Like many bands in the early development stage, they often practiced in front of friends and whoever else happened to be around. Frequently among the crowds that would gather was Freddie Mercury.

Freddie was already good friends with Staffell, and soon he was quite friendly with the group's drummer, Roger Taylor. Freddie and Roger hit it off well together since they had a mutual interest in Jimi Hendrix—a subject that Freddie could talk about for hours. While Freddie became a regular part of the group's entourage, they got their act together well enough to give themselves a name. The trio adopted the moniker of Smile. It was a simple, open-ended name with little meaning, but it seemed to suit the group well enough.

Soon enough, Smile was playing several gigs around town, during which Freddie was often in the audience. The first big break for Smile came on October 26, 1968, when they played alongside Pink Floyd. This event, though certainly memorable, perhaps sounds more impressive a feat than it actually was. As huge of an act as Pink Floyd would become by the late 1970s, they were still relatively obscure in the late 1960s.

After the Floyd gig, the group was booked to play a venue called the Royal Albert Hall, where they received favorable press coverage. In a tongue-in-cheek article, a reporter for *The Times* gleefully described Smile as "the loudest group in the Western World." Even without Freddie in the line-up, Brian May's guitar playing was no doubt getting attention.

Freddie meanwhile, though not in the band, had become a devoted member of the crew, riding along with the group to their shows and popping up wherever else they might be. Brian May later remembered how Freddie would counsel the group and give them unsolicited advice about stage presence and how to make their shows more dynamic. As Brian May later recalled, "He had this thing that we were presenting ourselves all wrong. He was into the show as a show, which was a pretty unusual idea in those days."

Smile continued to make waves and was eventually offered a one-single deal by Mercury Records. Some have noted the irony of Mercury Records being involved and have speculated that this is where Freddie got the idea to go by Mercury instead of his birth name of Bulsara. There is, however, no evidence to prove this was the case.

Freddie by this time had broken out with his own band, a group called Ibex. The group had some marginal success playing for small venues around town, but by the summer of 1969, Freddie became discouraged and felt that the group wasn't making the progress that it should. It was at this time that he consulted his bandmates and convinced them to change the name to Wreckage. In many ways, one could probably see the humor involved of these young men, many of them novices, naming their first major stab at music Wreckage, but despite the self-deprecating title, Freddie was serious in his aims for stardom.

It was an exciting time for many young British musicians as, just a few years prior, The Beatles had taken the world by storm. The Beatles were just four regular guys who went to an art school together and formed a band. Freddie Mercury very much wanted to do the same. Wreckage would soon end up in the trash heap, however, and after that, Freddie's stint in a group called Sour Milk Sea would prove even more short-lived. Freddie was then frustrated to learn that one of his former bandmates, Mike "Miffer" Smith, was engaging in trash talk behind his back.

In a letter dated October 26, 1969, Freddie fired off a letter to an acquaintance of his, Celine Daley, in which he complained about the situation. Freddie railed, "Miffer's not with us anymore cause the bastard just upped and left one morning saying he was going to be a milkman in Widnes. . . . Miffer, the sod, went and told everyone down here that I had seriously turned into a fully-fledged queer."

The language Freddie used might be offensive to modern-day sentiments, but times were a lot different back then. At any rate, Freddie's friends knew that he was a bit eccentric and flamboyant and would joke with him about it. A nickname tossed around by his bandmates in reference to

Freddie, in fact, was "the old queen." This was perhaps what would ultimately inspire the band name Queen years later.

But besides an occasional, good-natured ribbing, most of his friends didn't really think too much of it. Freddie was actually in a fairly serious relationship with a girl from Ealing—Rosemary Pearson—at the time. Rosemary would fondly recall the impression that Freddie made on her. She recalled, "He was charismatic, dressed outrageously—sometimes in shorts, no top and a fur coat—and was determined to make it as a singer. He was a clown, so much fun to be around. Freddie was also the only truly fearless person I ever met."

Rosemary and Freddie were soon inseparable and would go to art galleries, concerts, parties, and wherever else they pleased, arm in arm. Interestingly enough, it was Rosemary that first introduced Freddie to London's gay community. She had several gay friends, and Freddie showed an interest in getting to know them. His interest made his girlfriend a little hesitant, however, and as she later described it, "I felt that if he ever met these people, then that would be it. They would take him from me, and I would be shut out."

Rosemary and Freddie would eventually break up the following year. Not long after that, Freddie's latest musical outfit, Sour Milk Sea, also fell apart. Both his band and his girlfriend had broken up with him, but as sad and dejected as he felt, there was indeed a light at the end of the tunnel. Right around this time, Freddie received word that his friends in Smile were going through some changes of their own.

After intermittent squabbling with each other, their bassist and vocalist, Tim Staffell, decided to leave the group. Guitarist Brian May and drummer Roger Taylor now suddenly found themselves without a singer. Freddie Mercury saw a window of opportunity opening right in front of him, and he didn't hesitate to step through it.

Chapter Four

The Birth of Queen

"Onstage, I am a devil. But I'm hardly a social reject."

—Freddie Mercury

Freddie Mercury was like the missing puzzle piece that May and Taylor were looking for, and he quickly became the lead singer of the group in the summer of 1970. With Freddie taking on the role of frontman, the group began to practice together in London, with whoever could fill in on bass at the time. The band would eventually settle on a bassist by the name of Mike Grose.

Despite Brian and Roger's enthusiasm for Freddie, Grose would later recall that he wasn't too thrilled with Mercury's performance. As he later described, "I liked Tim's voice more than Freddie's. Tim was good, bloody good. Freddie used to sing flat. When he got to high notes, he would pull the microphone away from his mouth so you wouldn't quite hear him. But Brian used to talk to me about Freddie, and I think it was Brian who really believed in him at that stage."

This is a little surprising to hear, considering how much of a virtuoso singer Freddie Mercury would eventually become. At any rate, the four of them were soon regularly working on music together. Even though Freddie was the newbie to the band, he was sure to provide major input every step of the way.

Freddie not only provided his input on music but also on fashion. As Mike Grose would later recall, "Freddie and I went shopping for stage gear—I think on King's Road—and he got me into those black velvet trousers that were so tight I could hardly walk." For Freddie, every aspect of the band, from how they sounded to how they might look on stage, was important, and he was sure not to leave any detail out.

After all of the preparations had been made, the new line-up finally made its debut on June 27, 1970, at Truro City Hall. It was a venue that could support nearly a thousand people, but that night they were lucky to get just a couple hundred to show up. Neither the band nor the audience knew quite what would happen when they strutted out on stage, but it wouldn't be a disappointment. Emerging dressed in black with stack-heeled boots and several pieces of silver jewelry (all courtesy of Freddie), the group wowed the audience.

It was after this successful foray that Freddie would suggest changing the band's name to Queen. He received some pushback from his bandmembers at first, but ever-persistent, Mercury eventually brought them around to the idea. He would later explain the name choice by stating, "It's a strong name, very universal and immediate. It had a lot of visual potential and was open to all sorts of interpretations. I was certainly aware of gay connotations, but that was just one facet of it."

Such ambiguity would be a theme of Freddie Mercury's life. He never wanted anyone to think that they had completely figured him out, and he thrived on things that could have multiple meanings. This was also a way that he would connect to so many fans from various different backgrounds. This came naturally to Freddie; he loved to leave people guessing.

It was shortly after the band changed from Smile to Queen that Freddie decided to drop his last name of Bulsara for good, opting for the name "Mercury." The main reason that Freddie adopted this name was due to an early Queen song he produced by the name of "My Fairy King." In the song, Freddie sang, "Oh Mother Mercury, what have you done to me?" One day, Freddie unabashedly told his bandmates, "Well, I'm going to become Mercury because the mother in this song is my mother." Others have also noted some other possible influences such as the fact that in Greek mythology, Mercury is a messenger, and Freddie felt he had a message to impart.

Along with his new name and new band, Freddie Mercury also had a new girlfriend in the form of Mary Austin. Although Mary would later come to much the same realization as Freddie's previous girlfriend in regard to how committed he was to a monogamous heterosexual relationship, the two would remain friends for life.

Chapter Five

Queen's First Album

"We're a bit flashy, but the music's not one big noise."

—Freddie Mercury

By 1971, the final line-up of Queen was complete with the addition of bassist John Deacon. Deacon was only 19 years old at the time but already a prodigious bass player. Deacon had actually sat in at an early Queen show but wasn't too thrilled by what he saw. Deacon would later describe the moment he saw the band come out on stage, stating, "They were all dressed in black, and the lights were very dim too, so all I could see were four shadowy figures. They didn't make a lasting impression on me."

Regardless of his first impression, shortly thereafter, he would bump into Roger Taylor and Brian May and be informed that they were once again in the market for a bassist. Even though he had his reservations, when Brian invited him to try out, he went ahead and auditioned for the band. Brian, Freddie, and Roger immediately liked what they saw. They appreciated Deacon's style of playing, as well as his low-key personality. Deacon became an official member of the band in February of 1971, and he then went on to perform live with Queen for the first time on July 2 of that year.

It was with Deacon that the group would go on to record their first album—a self-titled piece that debuted in 1973. The members of Queen were quite fortunate in the arrangements the studio made for this recording; even though they were still a fairly obscure band, London's De Lane Lea Studios pulled out all the stops to make sure that Queen received the best the studio had to offer. The result was a complex, highly diverse arrangement that featured several facets of what would become the classic Queen sound. The album had ballads, it had theatrics, and it had hard-driving rock in which May's guitar sometimes seemed to borrow generously from the likes of Black Sabbath.

Although this album never managed to break out as a major success, it would always hold a place in the musicians' hearts. As Brian May thoughtfully recalled those days, "That album had the youth and freshness which was never regained, because you're only young once. It had a lot of rough edges . . . but obviously we didn't have the time to spend on it that we did subsequently. But I would never think of going back and redoing it, or anything like that, because I think it has a freshness we won't have again."

The album, after being shopped around by various record labels, was eventually picked up by EMI. In the meantime, the group was asked to perform at the BBC's Radio One program called *Sounds of the 70s*. In 1973, the seventies were still a rather young decade, and this program was determined to capitalize on what was hot at the moment. The gig wasn't paid, but it did provide a chance for the group to prove themselves, showing that they could hold their own.

After signing with EMI, which would produce their records in Britain, the group was then directed to Elektra Records, which would handle the production and distribution in the United States. Before Elektra signed on however, the managing director Jac Holzman wanted to see the band for himself. The occasion came on April 9, when the band was booked to perform at the Marquee Club. Here Freddie's antics were on full theatrical display.

As Brian May jammed out an instrumental interlude, Freddie came strutting out on stage dressed in a tight black catsuit. Skinny as a rail, Mercury proceeded to prance around before diving right into the band's set listing of songs for the night. If one gauged the performance solely from the music reviews that appeared afterward, it would seem as if the audience must have either loved it or hated it. One reviewer praised the group as being "Quite simply breathtaking! The band of the future!" Another one derided Freddie and company as nothing more than "a bunch of raving poofters trying to jump on the Bowie bandwagon while doing a poor piss-take of Black Sabbath."

Of course, when a new group comes out and is trying to find its groove, there will be plenty of naysayers who will claim that the band is ripping off an artist that had come before. During the early days of a band, primary influences are often the most evident. Brian May did indeed enjoy playing Black Sabbath-styled riffs, and sometimes it showed. But no matter what the critics may have said, the only person in the audience that really mattered that night was the managing director of Elektra, Jac Holzman—and Jac absolutely loved it.

Shortly after the group's performance at the Marquee, their first single was released on July 6, 1973. The track that hit the airwaves was "Keep Yourself Alive." It was a very apt title for a band that was still in survival mode, struggling to consolidate their gains in the music industry and stay alive in the business long enough to reach the next level. It was full steam ahead from here, and no matter what might happen next, Freddie Mercury knew that there was no going back.

Chapter Six

The Failed Australian Tour

"We've gone overboard on every Queen album. But that's Queen."

—Freddie Mercury

It wasn't long after the release of their first album that the band began working on their second, simply called *Queen II*. The band, taking what they learned the first time around about mastering music in the studio, went all out in their arrangements, creating epic musical narratives.

Unfortunately, since it was so close on the heels of their first album, it seemed to cast a shadow over what they had already done. It also proved to be a little bit distracting for the band since just as their first record was gaining traction, the members of Queen were completely immersed in a new one. Nevertheless, it was shortly after this latest album that the band was sent out on tour.

Their travels would eventually take them to France, Belgium, Holland, and Germany. The group then crisscrossed back to Britain to play at London's Paris Theatre, as well as a couple of high-energy performances at the group's old stomping ground of Imperial College—one of which would gain the distinction of becoming the band's first sold-out concert. Now, no matter what the critics might have said, sheer ticket sales were a clear indication that the band's music was catching on.

In January of 1974, Queen left home once again, this time for Melbourne, Australia, where they would play two gigs at the Sunbury Music Festival. Freddie started this journey in complete misery since due to a mishap with an inoculation—everyone in the group had to be inoculated before the trip—his arm became infected with gangrene. Mercury was also suffering from an acute case of tinnitus, which had compromised his hearing and led to no end of complaints. And Freddie wasn't the only one complaining; some of their hosts were a little less than satisfied as well.

During one performance in particular, one host made his own feelings clear. When introducing the group, he turned his back to a microphone, pulled his pants down, and then farted right into the mike. As this shocking little burst of methane coated the microphone, the host shouted, "That's what I think of those stuck-up Pommie bastards!"

Nevertheless, despite such debauched detractors, the show went quite well—that is until the overhead lighting decided to blow up, blacking out the whole platform on which the band performed. As it turns out, this was no accident either; the equipment was compromised by the Australian techs, who were upset because Queen had brought their own lighting guys rather than depending on their services.

With such abuse being hurled their way, Queen understandably canceled the next night's event, packed up, and went back to Britain. Making the bizarre experience in Australia even more surreal was the fact that the band was met with an army of reporters when they arrived at Heathrow Airport. The funny thing is that these reporters were not there to see the band—they were there to see the queen, as in Queen Elizabeth. As it turns out, someone had gotten confused and when they heard that Queen was flying in, they thought it was in reference to Queen Elizabeth's arrival. Nevertheless, Freddie tried to take advantage of the situation and, posing and pouting for photographers, he tried to assert himself as the only real queen in town. Soon the reporters got tired of the shenanigans, however, and dispersed.

Back in Britain, Freddie and the band were given more opportunity to raise their profile by presenting themselves to the *Top of the Pops*. This old British variety show brought in millions of viewers who tuned in to see Queen perform. In many ways, it was this performance that really paved the way for Queen's success. The instrumental powerhouse of Brian May, John Deacon, and Roger Taylor, with Freddie Mercury sauntering around at his theatrical best, was a captivating experience, one which *TheSunday Times* described as, "Led Zeppelin in frocks' contribution to glam-rock . . . pure Freddie Mercury, massively entertaining, superbly artificial and enigmatic to the point of meaninglessness!" That was a pretty hefty descriptor for the group, but one that summed it up nicely. The music was as powerful as Led

Zeppelin, yet interspersed with plenty of glam theatrics all the way.

Shortly after their *Top of the Pops* appearance, the band was on tour again. The tour started off well enough but was eventually marked by several riotous incidents. First, at a gig at Stirling University on March 16, 1974, a fight broke out in the crowd, leaving a couple of fans battered and bleeding from knife wounds. About a week after this, at an after-party held at the band's hotel on the Isle of Man, out-of-control party growers demolished the place. This resulted in the authorities issuing the band the proclamation, "We never want to see you or your people here again."

It was just a few weeks later that the band would wash up on American shores, starting the first leg of a tour that began in April. Their first gig was in Denver, Colorado, on April 16, where they opened for a band called Mott the Hoople. At first, they received some pushback from the Americans who didn't quite understand the concept of glam—for many, the group just seemed a little bit too odd for their tastes, as they hadn't seen anything quite like it before. Yet as Freddie warmed up the crowds, soon they liked it just as much as the British did back home.

It would turn out that Queen's biggest challenge in the United States would be when they showed up on Broadway. The fans here ran riot just as had happened on the Isle of Man, and after several people destroyed property, Queen was told to leave and not come back. Matters would soon get even worse, however, when guitarist Brian May unexpectedly passed out, stricken with an unknown ailment. Alarmed, May was checked out by physicians and was found to have contracted hepatitis.

It was believed that he had got it the same way that Freddie had contracted the gangrene infection—through the dirty needles that were used to inoculate them in Australia. In the midst of all of this disorder, the group made their way back to Britain, planning to revisit the U.S. the following year. In the meantime, Brian was laid up in the hospital for about four whole weeks before he recovered enough to be released.

That didn't mean that Brian May didn't keep himself busy because even while laid up in the hospital, he managed to get out his guitar and compose a few tunes that would end up on the latest Queen album, *Sheer Heart Attack*—an interesting title choice considering the circumstances of Brian May's faltering health.

Brian wasn't out of the hospital for very long before he got sick again. He had somehow suffered a perforated ulcer and needed an operation to keep from deteriorating. After the surgery, he seemed to recover well and was once again released from the hospital.

By the time September 5 rolled around, which just happened to be Freddie's birthday, the group was set to play at London's Café Royal. Freddie Mercury—frontman extraordinaire—was now 28 years old and felt as if he were on the top of the world. He had received all he could have ever asked for and more.

Chapter Seven

Breaking up with Mary Austin

"Years ago, I thought up the name Queen. It's just a name. But it's regal, obviously, and sounds splendid."

—Freddie Mercury

In the fall of 1974, Queen was back to touring around Britain. They kicked off this latest tour by performing at Manchester's Palace Theatre on October 30. The band typically opened up their performances with the lights turned off before Mercury appeared with a light shining down on him from above. Mercury would then begin singing while his bandmates continued to be shrouded in darkness. It was just as the music was beginning to build that the lights would kick on showing Brian May feverishly working the fretboard, Taylor pounding the drums, and Deacon plugging away at the bass. It was quite a sight to behold, and it was enhanced even further by the kind of special effects that had become so popular in the seventies, such as dry ice, fireworks, and special lighting effects.

It was while they were still out on this tour that the band's latest studio album, *Sheer Heart Attack*, came out. This album consisted of what would become a classic part of the Queen repertoire, with songs like "Flick of the Wrist" and, most especially, "Killer Queen." "Killer Queen" would reach number two on the U.K. charts, making it the band's first major hit.

Realizing their tendency to be a bit too grandiose, this album was scaled back considerably, giving audiences a rawer, more refreshing sound. The group had learned a lot while out on tour, and they had realized what an audience likes and what an audience doesn't— and this sort of empathy is obvious when one listens to *Sheer Heart Attack*. The album would eventually become platinum in the United Kingdom and gold in the United States.

It was on November 8, 1976, the day that the album was released, that Freddie Mercury had a near-disastrous mishap on stage. The band was playing in Glasgow, Scotland when some excited audience members thought it would be prudent to pull Mercury off stage and into the crowd. Freddie had apparently been inching closer and closer to the edge of the stage as if he were about to fall in, and the fans were more than happy to help him the rest of the way.

Freddie could have been seriously hurt, but fortunately he was able to get up from the fall mostly unphased. The seating section couldn't say the same, however, and due to this debacle and other mayhem that night, it's said that ten whole rows of seats were trashed. This seemed to be a repeat of Queen's misadventures on Broadway and the Isle of Man, and the band was probably expecting to have to once again pay for the destruction that had been wrought.

Yet this time, things were different. Instead of receiving a bill, they were each handed a silver statuette out of gratitude for packing the place full of concert-goers. This was apparently the first time that the venue had had a full house and, despite the damage, they were very appreciative of that fact.

The band was prodigiously busy during this period and was always on the move. In late November, they played to another packed house at the Rainbow in London. Close on the heels of this extravaganza, they then rushed off to play abroad in Sweden, Finland, Belgium, Holland, Germany, and Spain. If anyone in the band had harbored any lingering doubts as to whether or not the group would be successful, they were gone at this point.

Guitarist Brian May, who had been in and out of school during the rise of Queen, gave up his coursework for good as a testament to the fact that he was now hedging all of his bets on the band. John Deacon found himself settling in for the long haul as well and felt secure enough to marry his fiancé, Veronica Tetzlaff. Freddie Mercury meanwhile was becoming increasingly involved with his sweetheart, Mary Austin.

Freddie had already asked Mary to marry him a few years prior. It was a stunning spectacle on Christmas Day 1973 when Freddie handed over a giant gift box to Mary. This box was just a decoy because once opened, there was yet another package inside. When this package was opened, there was another one—and so it went until Mary reached a tiny box that had a beautiful ring inside.

Mary, feeling entirely overwhelmed, asked Freddie what she should do with it. He told her to put it on and proposed that the two should get married. Mary was stunned but found herself in agreement, and the two were engaged. This engagement, however, would drag on for years with no end in sight. As Freddie's star continued to rise, he became more and more absorbed in the wild persona he was crafting. With it came many admirers, including other men that he would have romantic flings with.

Mary knew that something wasn't quite right in their relationship and eventually felt compelled to address the situation, with Mercury telling her that it felt like he had a noose around his neck, as if she were somehow holding him back from who he really was. It's said that Freddie then came clean and opened up to her about being bisexual.

Mary later recalled that his acknowledgment of this part of his life came as a relief. Even though she already suspected as much, it soothed her conscience to have him confirm what she was feeling. As Mary described it, "It was a relief really, to actually hear it from him. To know that I had guessed more or less right." Mary then went on to state, "I was supportive of him becoming gay because it was part of himself. It was nice to see Freddie at one with himself. It was more than nice. It was wonderful."

Freddie Mercury didn't want to part from Mary, but she felt she had no choice. She felt that if she didn't let go, she would be holding him back, and thus, Mary ended their engagement in December of 1976, about three years after it had begun. It was the end of a long personal struggle Freddie had been having between his own identity and a woman he cherished. Many fans believe that this struggle was in large part expressed in the epic Queen song "Bohemian Rhapsody," which appeared on the band's album *A Night at the Opera* that came out around this time.

The song opens with Freddie asking, "Is this the real life? Is this just fantasy? Caught in a landslide. No escape from reality." It has been interpreted that with these lyrics, Freddie was speaking to his own insecurities over what aspect of his life was really real. What was his real life? Was it his quiet relationship with Mary or the extravagant lifestyle he engaged in on the road?

A little bit later in the song, Mercury then seems to lament having gone too far and not being able to go back, or as he mournfully crooned, "Mama, life had just begun, but now I've gone and thrown it all away." It's been speculated that the "Mama" Freddie refers to is actually Mary Austin. Perhaps he felt his potential life with her had just begun, but all that promise of whatever they could have had together had been "thrown away."

In the next verse, Freddie then goes on to say, "Didn't mean to make you cry. If I'm not back again this time tomorrow, Carry on, carry on." This could be interpreted as Freddy telling Mary that if he drifts too far away from what he had with her, she's free to carry on without him. The next set of verses seems to enshrine this sentiment, as Freddie confirms, "Too late, my time has come, Sends shivers down my spine, body's aching all the time. Goodbye, everybody, I've got to go. Gotta leave you all behind and face the truth." For some, this truth was Freddie facing the true lifestyle he was drawn to and leaving the facade of his relationship with Mary behind.

Of course, this is just one interpretation, and the actual deeper meaning of the song has always been a mystery. Freddie Mercury himself was always vague and evasive when asked about it. At one point, he simply generalized that the theme of the song is about "relationships." At any rate, this plaintive narrative about transition, change, and leaving the past behind seemed to serve as the perfect soundtrack for Mercury's mindset at the time as he embarked upon the next great phase of his life.

Chapter Eight

The Magic of Mercury

*"The reason we're successful, darling? My
overall charisma, of course."*

—Freddie Mercury

Queen's album *Night at the Opera* made them
bona fide stars, and the epic song "Bohemian
Rhapsody" became the group's first number one
single in Britain. The album also went platinum in
the United States, signifying Queen's greatest
success yet in North America.

The album was then closely followed by a
1976 release called *A Day at the Races*. This
album featured high-soaring hits such as
"Somebody to Love" and "Tie Your Mother
Down." Yet it would be 1977's *News of the
World* that would completely steal the show. This
album would house Queen's arguably most
recognizable hits of all time: "We Will Rock
You" and "We Are the Champions."

The song "We Will Rock You" is about as iconic as it can get and can be heard to this day not only on the radio but at just about any gathering where a lot of people are present. It's been a favorite soundtrack for sporting events and other occasions where spectators can clap their hands and stomp their feet to that unforgettable drum beat.

The lyrics to this song did not originate from Freddie Mercury but came by way of Queen's guitarist Brian May. It's said that Brian was inspired to write the song after he had a dream about music that the audience could participate in. That's exactly what this track does for people. Freddie's vocalized invitation of "Sing it!" followed by the chorus, "We will, we will, rock you, rock you," does indeed serve as a grand invitation for the audience to take part in the song.

On the album *News of the World*, the song "We Will Rock You" is immediately followed by the track "We Are the Champions." The two songs were made to segue together. Even though they are distinctly separate entities, the two tracks have long since been associated with each other, and Queen would typically play them back to back during live concerts.

The year 1977 was an interesting time in music, most especially in Britain where a new form of music called punk rock was taking shape under the guidance of bands like the Sex Pistols. Interestingly enough, it was while Queen was recording "We Will Rock You" that they had a direct run-in with none other than Sex Pistols' bass player, Sid Vicious.

The Pistols were actually booked to do some recordings at the studio around the same time. The band would later recall how Sid took it upon himself to berate Freddie Mercury. Sid apparently didn't appreciate the finer tastes of Queen's frontman and openly mocked him, asking Freddie if he had "brought ballet to the masses yet?" As much as Freddie was able to show a softer, gentler side, he was not someone easily pushed around. He demonstrated this fact handily by throwing Sid out of the studio.

Nevertheless, it has long been speculated over whether or not strains of this new punk sound may have leaked into *News of the World*. The frenetic energy of "We Will Rock You" does seem to have some punk elements, as well as some would argue even a trace of hip hop in Freddie's rapid vocal delivery.

The late seventies was undoubtedly a time of great musical experimentation and transition. Right around this time, punk, reggae, hip-hop, disco, and many other new forms of music were gaining steam, and Queen was ready to delve into it all. Their next album, titled simply *Jazz*, seemed to speak to this build-up of influences.

This work was followed up by a live album in 1979 called *Live Killers*. The live album documented the group's dogged touring of Europe. One of the perhaps most memorable moments of Mercury in Europe was in Madrid, Spain when Freddie—ever the showman—faced a tough crowd. Getting frustrated with the anaemic response of the audience, he tried to encourage them by raising the champagne glass (Freddie loved to drink champagne on stage) he was holding to give an impromptu toast to the crowd. He spoke a few words of good will in what little Spanish he knew, hoping to get a response from the audience.

When he was met with yawns and blank empty stars, Freddie uncharacteristically became angry with the crowd and, pouring his drink out on people down below, shouted, "Take that! That's for being Spanish!" A harsh move to be sure, but this bit of venom actually seemed to do the trick. Shortly thereafter, the audience was screaming and shouting, really getting into the music.

Seemingly reassured, Freddie then sat down at the piano to play some softer numbers. Before doing so, he banged his hand on the closed piano lid and was heard exclaiming in triumph, "That's the way to do it!" Freddie may have been momentarily discouraged, but even with a tough crowd, he knew how to rebound and eventually get them on his side before the night was over. This was simply the magic of Mercury at work.

Chapter Nine

Live Aid and Mercury's Final Years

"Who wants to live forever?"

—Freddie Mercury

As the 1970s turned into the 1980s, Queen was at the top of their game. Their first album of the decade, aptly titled *The Game*, seemed to be a confirmation of them having reached this pinnacle of success. This album featured the unforgettable track "Another One Bites the Dust," which would be another of Queen's greatest hits of all time.

Not only that, this song could be said to be a major theme of the 1980s in general with its almost hip-hop beat and infectious lyrics. Freddie can't lay claim to the words of this song, which were written by Queen's bassist, John Deacon. As hard-driving as this song was, the last half of the album provides older fans with some classic

Queen tunes, in the stylings of "Play the Game," "Sail Away Sweet Sister," and "Save Me."

One of the most surprising and intriguing tracks from this album is a number called "Don't Try Suicide." Although the music itself is upbeat, the lyrics offer a stark warning about not becoming self-absorbed and doing something one might regret. In the end, *The Game* presents itself as the album Queen hoped would bridge the divide between where they were in the 1970s and where they hoped to go in the 1980s.

Not long after this album, Queen's ability to make huge record sales began to decline. They were nevertheless still big concert draws and continued to perform for packed venues throughout the early 1980s. Being the ultimate stadium rock band that they were, it was then only natural that Queen would be summoned to perform at the iconic Live Aid benefit concert in 1985.

Live Aid was an idea developed by singer-songwriter Bob Geldof, who was inspired to help famine-stricken Ethiopia. The East African nation of Ethiopia was being administered by the communist regime of Mengistu Haile Mariam at the time. Mengistu had overthrown the long-reigning monarch of Ethiopia, Emperor Haile

Selassie, in 1976, and the communists had ruled with an iron fist ever since. The Mengistu government's communist, centralized planning didn't work out too well for the people, however, and was made even worse by a massive famine that lasted from 1983 to 1985. It was this famine that Geldof was seeking to render aid to, using live music as a means of fundraising for the cause.

Upon being told of their invitation to play for Live Aid, Freddie Mercury and the band didn't hesitate to answer the call. The group was just coming off a major tour for their latest album, the 1984 record called *The Works*. Seemingly not even taking a break, they then dived right into the business of performing before 70,000 fans at Wembley Stadium in England, while 90,000 more watched via satellite from a stadium in Philadelphia—not to mention the 2 billion people who tuned in to watch the spectacle on television.

Although it all came together more or less by chance, it was a moment that Freddie Mercury no doubt had always dreamed about. Here was his chance to show the world once and for all just what a showman he could be—and he didn't disappoint. On the day of the concert, on July 13, 1985, it would be Queen—and most especially

Mercury—who would be remembered more than anyone else. "Bohemian Rhapsody" had the fans spellbound, and "We Will Rock You" had them up on their feet, stomping, clapping, and chanting right along with Freddie.

After Live Aid, the group would forge a new album called *A Kind of Magic*, which was released in 1986. The band then embarked upon yet another whirlwind tour shortly thereafter. One of the most iconic stops on this tour was a gig that Queen played in Budapest, Hungary. Here they performed to 80,000 fans behind the Iron Curtain that separated the East from the West. Before the Berlin Wall had even come down, Freddie was doing what he could to bring the thrilling freedom of rock music to the Eastern Bloc masses. Freddie wowed the crowd with all of Queen's greatest hits as well as doing his own rendition of a Hungarian folk song.

Sadly, it was shortly after this triumphant run that Mercury would receive the terrible news that he had been infected with HIV. Freddie is said to have been diagnosed with the illness in the spring of 1987. He tried to keep his diagnosis secret, but the media doggedly pursued him over the years, trying to get to the bottom of it. When Freddie became visibly thinner and weaker as the months progressed, their inquest only increased.

The stories were only magnified by alleged former acquaintances who fueled the rumor mill with stories about Freddie being in denial about having HIV. In the meantime, Freddie began to shy away from public engagements. He would ultimately make his final live appearance in 1990 at the Dominion Theatre in London, where he joined the other members of Queen to accept the Brit Award for Outstanding Contribution to British Music.

Just a little over a year later, the megastar the world came to know as Freddie Mercury would be gone.

Conclusion

Freddie's condition had greatly deteriorated by 1991, but he still felt he had work to do. Around this time, he embarked upon what would be his final studio recordings with Queen. Freddie was said to have been in good spirits despite his obvious battle with illness and even cracked jokes at the time. He told those around him that he didn't want to focus on the disease that had racked his body but just wanted to make good music one last time. It must have been a strangely surreal feeling for his old bandmates, knowing that these last few sessions were most likely the final time that they would play together.

Freddie gave his all during these takes, and one song in particular, called "These Are the Days of Our Lives," was filled with heart-wrenching emotion. The song is said to be about Freddie's goodbye to his fans and essentially all whom he loved. The song ends with a somber and reflective Freddie affirming, "I still love you."

These final recordings were wrapped up in June of 1991. With their conclusion, Mercury went back to his home in London, where he tried to make the best of the last few months he had left. He eventually passed away surrounded by friends and family on November 24, 1991, at age 45. His long-term partner, Jim Hutton, was right by his side. Freddie had done much with his life, but one can only wonder what more there might have been had he lived longer.

Freddie Mercury has a special place in the hearts of many, and even though he's gone, the magic that he brought us through his music continues to live on.

Bibliography

Bret, David (2014). *Freddie Mercury: An Intimate Biography*.

Clarke, Ross (1991). *Freddie Mercury: A Kind of Magic*.

Jackson, Laura (1997). *Freddie Mercury: The Biography*.

Langthorne, Mark & Richards, Matt (2016). *Somebody to Love: The Life, Death and Legacy of Freddie Mercury*.

Popoff, Martin (2018). *Queen: Album by Album*.

Taraporevala, Sooni (2004). *Parsis: The Zoroastrians of India: A Photographic Journey*.

Printed in Great Britain
by Amazon